Fabulous Fall Mini Coloring Book 1

30 Fabulous Fall Designs with Less detail for coloring in.

By Artist Dwyanna Stoltzfus

Copyright © 2017 by Dwyanna Stoltzfus

ALL RIGHTS RESERVED

ISBN-10:1976505127

ISBN-13:978-1976505126

This publication is for personal use only.
No part of this publication may be reproduced, stored in a retrieval
System, or transmitted in any form or by any means – electronic, mechanical, photocopy,
Or any other - without the written permission
of the artist/publisher – Dwyanna Stoltzfus.

Unauthorized reproduction of any part of this publication by any means
Is an infringement of copyright.
All artwork and images in this publication are
Protected by copyright laws.

Join the Fun!!

Share your colored pages!!

You are invited to color the pages
From this and all publications by
Dwyanna Stoltzfus. Then scan and post
Your colored creations in
Coloring with Dwyanna
Adult Coloring Group
On facebook
https://web.facebook.com/groups/1519357628356169/?_rdr
Join Coloring with Dwyanna Coloring Group,
And have fun sharing your colored pages
And meeting new coloring friends.
Members of the group will also have access
To free coloring pages.
You are welcome to share your colored pages on
Any social network, make sure to mention the title of
The book and the author/artist name.
Uncolored images may not be shared.

Check out my blog at:

coloringwithdwyanna.blogspot.com

PDF Printable coloring pages available

On Etsy at

https://www.etsy.com/people/dwyannastoltzfus

Follow Dwyanna's art on facebook at

Oodles of Doodles Designs –

Adult Coloring Books by

Dwyanna Stoltzfus

https://web.facebook.com/Oodles-of-Doodles-Designs-Adult-Coloring-Books-by-Dwyanna-Stoltzfus-743502922387046/

About:

Get ready to color 30 fabulous fall designs by Artist Dwyanna Stoltzfus.

This mini edition is only 6X9 inches. The perfect size to take along!

In this adult coloring book you will find 30 beautiful illustrations, printed one per page.

A collection of wonderful images for those who prefer less detail when coloring.

In this book you will find lots of pumpkins, apples, leaves, mandalas, sunflowers, girls, and more!

You can use this coloring book to help you relax and unwind after a long day.

Or you can use it just for fun. You can color the designs simply or add depth and creativity by shading and highlighting.

Crayons can be used on most of the designs in this book.

You can also color with fine tip markers, gel pens, and colored pencils.

Enjoy the experience of coloring!!

But most of all relax and have fun!!

Coloring tips:

If you desire to add depth to your coloring you can shade with colored pencils.

Use dark colors around edges and into the peaks. Blend in light colors for the middle and more open spaces. You can use black to darken areas, and white to lighten and brighten areas.

Acknowledgments

Thank You to my family for all your support
of my art and this project.
I could not have done it without you!!

Thank You God for the gift and love
Of art and drawing!!

© Copyright 2017 Dwyanna Stoltzfus

© Copyright 2017 Dwyanna Stoltzfus

www.ingramcontent.com/pod-product-compliance
Lightning Source LLC
Chambersburg PA
CBHW050018230526
45470CB00003B/1030